ROBOTS' REVENGE

CLIVE GIFFORD

QEB Publishing

Cover Design: Rosie Levine
Illustrator: Damien Jones
Editor: Amanda Askew
Designer: Punch Bowl Design
QEB Project Editor: Ruth Symons
Art Director: Laura Roberts-Jensen
Editorial Director: Victoria Garrard

Picture credits (t=top, b=bottom, l=left,
r=right, c=center)

Alamy 5b © GL Archive / Alamy, 18t ©
FLPA / Alamy, 26t © RGB Ventures LLC dba
SuperStock / Alamy, 27t © RGB Ventures
LLC dba SuperStock / Alamy, 41b © Hugh
Threlfall / Alamy; **Science Photo Library** 5t
DAVID DUCROS/SCIENCE PHOTO LIBRARY,
31 NASA/CARNEGIE MELLON UNIVERSITY/
SCIENCE PHOTO LIBRARY; **Shutterstock**
48l Brian A Jackson, 44b Maxx-Studio,
46b Tomas Mikula, 47t Monika Wisniewska,
47b Yu Lan

Copyright © QEB Publishing 2014

First published in the US in 2014
by QEB Publishing, Inc.
3 Wrigley, Suite A, Irvine, CA 92618

www.qed-publishing.co.uk

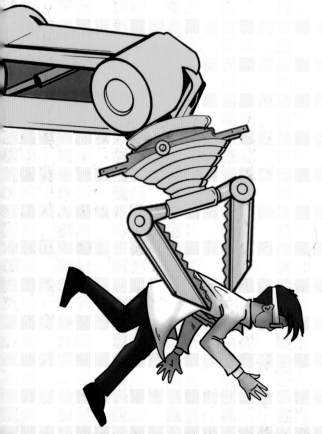

A CIP record for this book is available
from the Library of Congress.

ISBN 978 1 60992 622 9

Printed in China

How to begin your adventure

Are you ready for an awesome adventure in which you must solve mind-bending puzzles? Then you've come to the right place!

Robots' Revenge isn't an ordinary book—you don't read the pages in order, 1, 2, 3. . . Instead you jump forward and backward through the book as you face a series of challenges. Sometimes you may lose your way, but the story will always guide you back to where you need to be.

The story starts on page 4. Straight away, there are questions to answer and problems to overcome. The questions will look something like this:

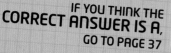 **IF YOU THINK THE CORRECT ANSWER IS A, GO TO PAGE 37**

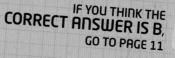 **IF YOU THINK THE CORRECT ANSWER IS B, GO TO PAGE 11**

Your task is to solve each problem. If you think the correct answer is A, turn to page 37 and look for the same symbol in red. That's where you will find the next part of the story.

If you make the wrong choice, the text will explain where you went wrong and let you have another chance.

The problems in this book are about robotics and inventions. To solve them, you must use your knowledge and common sense. To help you, there's a glossary of useful words at the back of the book, starting on page 44.

ARE YOU READY?
Turn the page and let your adventure begin!

ROBOTS' REVENGE

Buzzzz! A robot flies past your head. You arrive at Engleby's Inventorium, where you're working as an apprentice. You haven't yet managed to meet the genius inventor Edison Engleby, so you turn up early one morning, hoping to catch him.

BUT WHAT DOES THE DAY HAVE IN STORE FOR YOU? TURN TO PAGE 9 TO FIND OUT.

No, 111 isn't right. In binary, you can add a 1 to a column if there was a 0 there before. To add a 1 to a column already containing a 1, change that 1 to a 0 and add the 1 to a new column on the left.

1	0001
2	0010
3	?
4	0100
5	0101
6	0110

TRY AGAIN
ON PAGE 17

That's not right. Cassini-Huygens is a robotic spacecraft that was sent to explore Saturn and its moons in 1997.

GO BACK TO PAGE 23 AND TRY AGAIN

Yes, underwater robots such as Kaikō and Nereus have reached the deepest part of the Pacific Ocean, more than six miles (10,000 meters) below sea level.

Engleby continues: *"You need to get the master keys from inside the Inventors' Hall."*

Engleby is surprisingly relaxed considering the peril you're in! You head down the corridor to the hall, but the door is locked. You touch a computer screen mounted on the wall and a man appears.

I am Thomas Edison. To open the door, answer this question: Which of these did I invent?

INVENTORS' HALL

Three pictures appear. Which one do you choose?

THE CARBON MICROPHONE
GO TO PAGE 24

THE LIGHT BULB
JUMP TO PAGE 13

THE MODERN, BAGLESS VACUUM CLEANER
FLIP TO PAGE 41

That's right. Unimate, the first industrial robot arm, did a tough job—it handled red-hot steel used to make cars—but that was in a factory rather than a danger zone.

The tank contains three AUVs. Each has a maximum depth it can dive to safely. You see REX in a pod about 333 feet (100 meters) down.

Which AUV do you choose to retrieve the pod?

Super Sub	Ocean Navigator	Deep Explorer
Dive rate:	**Dive rate:**	**Dive rate:**
264 feet (80 meters) per minute	165 feet (50 meters) per minute	16.5 feet (5 meters) per minute
Max depth:	**Max depth:**	**Max depth:**
116 psi (8 bar)	174 psi (12 bar)	580 psi (40 bar)
GO TO PAGE 16	TRAVEL TO PAGE 23	FLIP TO PAGE 38

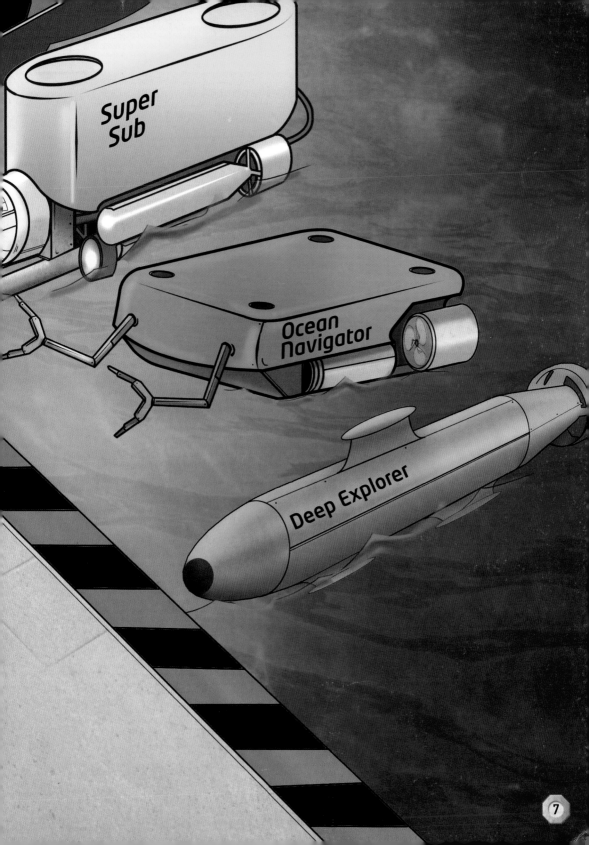

You're right! A prototype is the original version of an invention.

Why would anyone want to destroy Engleby's prototypes?

You wait for the two figures to leave, then try the door—but it's locked. You notice another door that says, **"PRIVATE. DO NOT ENTER."** There's a keypad next to it, and a question flashing on a screen.

What number do you enter?

1974
GO TO
PAGE 41

1944
HEAD OVER
TO PAGE 26

1999
FLIP TO
PAGE 18

PRIVATE. DO NOT ENTER.

SECURITY CODE

Enter code: In which year did Ernő Rubik make the first prototype of the Rubik's Cube?

Yes! Mary Anderson invented car windshield wipers, Tabitha Babbitt invented the circular saw, and Stephanie Kwolek invented Kevlar—a strong material used for body armor and helmets.

Behind the exhibit is a panel, protected under a thick slab of glass that's far too heavy for you to lift. There's a large robot arm beside it, with some end effectors.

Which end effector do you fit to the robot to lift the glass?

MAGNETIC GRIPPER
GO TO PAGE 21

VACUUM SUCTION PADS
HEAD TO PAGE 17

STEEL CLAW
TRAVEL TO PAGE 30

You wander into the main lab. Ena Vayshon, the head technician, is working on a new robot design.

What are you doing here so early? Not snooping around, I hope!

Mr. Engleby hasn't been seen for weeks. Not since the chief designer, Hugh Reeka, left. But you can help me. Hand me the silicon chip that carries out instructions—not one that stores data.

No! I was hoping to meet Mr. Engleby to talk to him about my ideas.

Which chip do you pass to her?

RAM CHIPS

RAM
GO TO PAGE 13

ROM CHIPS

ROM
TURN TO PAGE 36

CPU CHIPS

CPU
HEAD OVER TO PAGE 21

 No. Whitcomb L. Judson invented the first basic zipper in the 1890s.

TRY AGAIN
ON PAGE 18

 No, aluminum is a single metal. An alloy is a combination of more than one metal, or metal and carbon.

RETURN TO PAGE 20 AND TRY AGAIN

No way! An MAV is a micro air vehicle—a robotic mini aircraft.

GO BACK TO PAGE 16 AND TRY AGAIN

 If the robot had video cameras, it wouldn't notice any sound you made.

TRY AGAIN
ON PAGE 30

 B Activating switch B alone won't complete the circuit.

TRY AGAIN
ON PAGE 32

 Correct. An electric current that flows through an electrical circuit is measured in amps, short for amperes.

At the end of the passage are three hatches, each made of a different metal. You tell Engleby and again he gives you a quiz!

Inventors learn to solve problems by breaking them down into small steps. Computers work in this way too, and convert instructions down to just two numbers. What are these two numbers?

2 AND 5
GO TO PAGE 41

1 AND 0
GO TO PAGE 20

AFFIRMATIVE. THERE ARE MORE THAN SIX MILLION IN SERVICE. I AM EDNA, ENGLEBY'S DEXTROUS, NIMBLE ASSISTANT. AT YOUR SERVICE.

You step into a room full of books and papers. Napping in a corner is Edison Engleby, who wakes up with a start!

You quickly tell him about the Superbots that are patroling the factory, and the Power Surger that will fry the factory's circuits in less than an hour!

Wowzers! What an adventure! Don't worry—they're no match for my inventive genius. Let me think of a plan . . .

He stands there for five minutes, muttering to himself before collecting parts from around the room.

WHAT IS HE UP TO? FIND OUT HIS PLAN ON PAGE 23

Afraid not. That's the symbol for an **OR** gate. An **OR** gate gives out a high signal if either of its inputs are a high signal too.

HIGH SIGNAL → OR → HIGH SIGNAL
LOW SIGNAL →

TRY AGAIN ON PAGE 26

Iron is a single metal, not an alloy, which is a mixture of metals.

TRY AGAIN ON PAGE 20

Correct. The soldering iron melts some solder and allows Engleby to join the wire to the panel.

Wonderful! Hand me the card with the largest memory. This will make sure the tablet can run the communications program, so we can talk to each other.

What do you give him?

memory card	memory card	memory card
1,000 MB capacity	**500 GB** capacity	**4 TB** capacity

MOVE TO PAGE 19

JUMP TO PAGE 31

GO TO PAGE 37

Roll turns the whole cube around but the front face doesn't match up.

TRY AGAIN ON PAGE 38

No! REX's cutters slice through thin air!

YOU MUST TRY AGAIN ON PAGE 22

ROTATE ROLL

No, not exactly. Humphry Davy invented the first electric light bulb in 1809. However, Thomas Edison produced the first practical light bulb that sold in large numbers.

HEAD BACK TO PAGE 5

No, RAM stands for random-access memory. It allows stored data to be accessed in any order at all but it doesn't carry out instructions.

TRY AGAIN ON PAGE 9

Spot on! AUV stands for autonomous underwater vehicle. This is a type of robot that can navigate its own way to a target.

You leave the tablet recharging under a light and go to the tank.

On the side of the tank is a computer screen demanding a password to operate the AUVs.

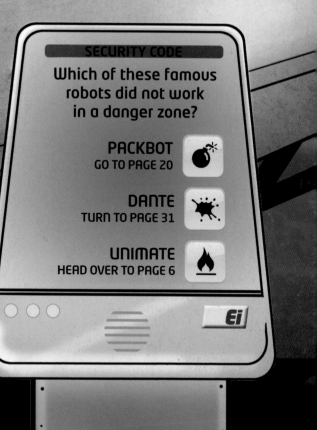

SECURITY CODE

Which of these famous robots did not work in a danger zone?

PACKBOT
GO TO PAGE 20

DANTE
TURN TO PAGE 31

UNIMATE
HEAD OVER TO PAGE 6

Ei

Right on! Wind tunnels are used to measure streamlining—how smoothly air flows around new vehicles and other inventions. A more streamlined machine can often go faster or use less fuel. Testing is important because it makes sure the robot works in the best way.

You make your way across the factory floor, past dozens of robots all working together on the assembly line. Suddenly one of the robots drops a part. Then another, and another. The assembly line is out of control!

Frightened, you duck as a robot arm swings right past your head. Then your breath is taken away as a robot arm lifts you off your feet!

It swings you around and drops you onto an automated guided vehicle (AGV). This type of robot normally ferries parts and materials around the factory, but now it's carrying you at high speed toward a wall of crates!

FRICTION

MINIMUM   MAXIMUM

You look for a stop button, but all you can find is a lever labeled FRICTION.

Which way do you move it?

TOWARD
MINIMUM
TURN OVER TO PAGE 33

TOWARD
MAXIMUM
SPEED ON TO PAGE 39

Correct! Many robots have a drive system, so they can move their parts.

You have been studying! Try this one: Robots have tools added, so they can do certain tasks. What are these tools called?

ACTUATORS
GO TO PAGE 20

END EFFECTORS
FLIP TO PAGE 27

GO TO PAGE 20

FLIP TO PAGE 27

For every 33 feet (10 meters) a robot sub descends, the pressure increases by 14.5 psi (pounds per square inch) or 1 bar. At great depths, an unprotected robot sub will be crushed like a tin can. This robot won't dive below 265 feet (80 meters).

14.5 psi or 1 bar = 33 feet (10 meters) depth
? psi or ? bar = 333 feet (100 meters) depth

RETURN TO PAGE 6 AND **TRY AGAIN**

RETURN TO PAGE 6 AND TRY AGAIN

If you go to the main doors, you could be walking straight into danger.

GO BACK TO PAGE 29 AND **TRY AGAIN**

GO BACK TO PAGE 29 AND TRY AGAIN

You're right! Stainless steel is an alloy, or mixture, of iron, carbon, and chromium.

You slide through the hatch and drop into the Deepwater Tank room. At the end of the room, a robot scuttles into view. You need to tell Engleby about it.

What type of robot is it?

AGV
MOVE TO PAGE 26

MAV
JUMP TO PAGE 9

SWARM ROBOT
HEAD TO PAGE 30

MOVE TO PAGE 26

JUMP TO PAGE 9

HEAD TO PAGE 30

Bingo! The vacuum suction pads stick firmly on to the glass, allowing the robot arm to lift it up. You grab the smart key and Engleby tells you to go to the **AND/OR/NOT Room** on the far side of the building. A map appears on the tablet screen.

There are 3 routes to the **AND/OR/NOT Room**, but Superbots are lurking everywhere.

To find the best route, answer this question:

= Superbots

Inventors' Hall

How is the number 3 shown in the binary number system?

3   11   111

store room

AND/OR/NOT ROOM

FLIP TO PAGE 5

TURN TO PAGE 26

GO TO PAGE 42

main laboratory

wind tunnel

sales office

stairs

Ei

smart key

No! The Rubik's Cube was 25 years old in 1999.

HAVE ANOTHER TRY ON PAGE 8

 Good choice. Sonic sensors can only pick up sound, so you stand quietly until it crawls out of the room.

Engleby appears on the tablet.

Seed hooks from Burdock plant

 Many inventions are inspired by nature. George de Mestral noticed how certain plant seeds hooked into his dog's fur. Do you know what it inspired him to invent?

You don't have time for this, but try to answer politely.

ZIPPERS
JUMP TO PAGE 9

VELCRO
GO TO PAGE 43

SUPERGLUE
HEAD OVER TO PAGE 36

C No, the Post-it note was invented by Arthur Fry in the 1970s, the Frisbee was invented by Walter Frederick Morrison in the 1930s, and the slinky was invented by Richard James in 1943.

GO BACK TO PAGE 24 AND **TRY AGAIN**

Yellow hydraulic fluid spills out of the pipe but the pneumatic-powered robot is still moving.

HEAD BACK TO PAGE 40 AND **TRY AGAIN**

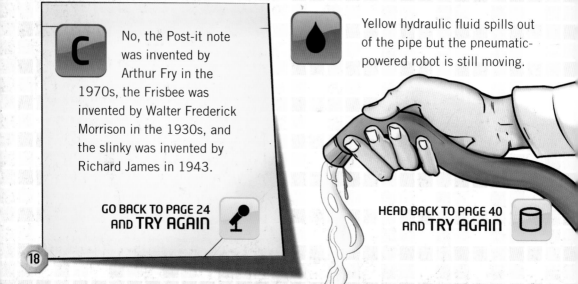

No, a prototype is needed to test an invention before it becomes a final design.

GO BACK TO PAGE 39 AND **THINK AGAIN**

No! MB stands for megabyte. 1,000 megabytes equal 1 gigabyte (GB), so it's not the largest memory card.

TRY AGAIN ON PAGE 12

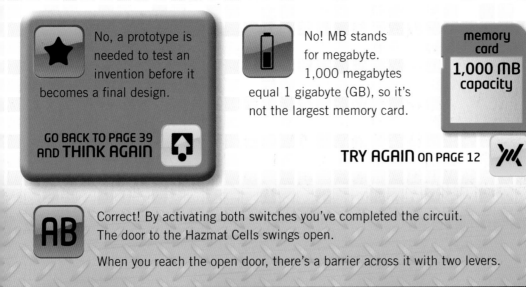
memory card
1,000 MB capacity

AB Correct! By activating both switches you've completed the circuit. The door to the Hazmat Cells swings open.

When you reach the open door, there's a barrier across it with two levers.

You completed the circuit, but what kind of logic gate did it act like?

Gulp! This is a tough test! Which lever do you pull?

AND LOGIC GATE
GO TO PAGE 29

OR LOGIC GATE
TURN TO PAGE 33

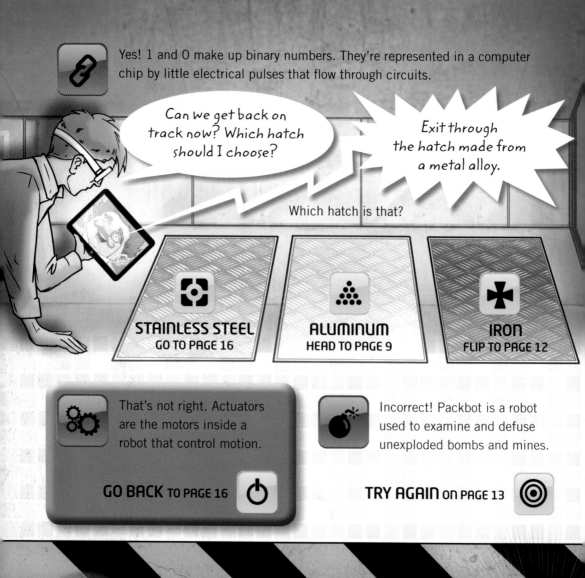

Yes! 1 and 0 make up binary numbers. They're represented in a computer chip by little electrical pulses that flow through circuits.

Can we get back on track now? Which hatch should I choose?

Exit through the hatch made from a metal alloy.

Which hatch is that?

STAINLESS STEEL
GO TO PAGE 16

ALUMINUM
HEAD TO PAGE 9

IRON
FLIP TO PAGE 12

That's not right. Actuators are the motors inside a robot that control motion.

GO BACK TO PAGE 16

Incorrect! Packbot is a robot used to examine and defuse unexploded bombs and mines.

TRY AGAIN ON PAGE 13

YES! Using yaw, REX's gripper lines up the red squares on the front face of the cube.

A siren blasts, exits open, the power circuits around the building shut down, and emergency lighting kicks in. The Power Surger won't work, so the factory is saved!

You start retracing your steps back to Engleby's lab, but as you round a corner, a terrifying sight causes you to scream.

TURN TO PAGE 28 TO FIND OUT WHAT'S IN STORE

Incorrect. Psi is used to measure pressure. 14.5 psi (or 1 bar) is equal to the pressure that Earth's atmosphere presses down on the planet.

PICK A **DIFFERENT PASSAGE** ON PAGE 37

While useful for picking up iron and steel objects, a magnet cannot attract glass.

TRY AGAIN ON PAGE 8 **A**

Well done! CPU stands for central processing unit. It's a chip that carries out instructions given to it by computer programs.

Ena smiles warmly. Now's your chance to find out what happened.

Why did the chief designer leave?

He was fired for trying to sell our inventions to another company. Engleby was devastated.

So, you're an apprentice? Let's see what you've learned so far. What does a robot's drive system do?

IT POWERS **MOVEMENT.**
HEAD OVER TO PAGE 16

IT CONTAINS ALL OF THE ROBOT'S **SENSORS.**
GO TO PAGE 31

IT GIVES THE ROBOT **INTELLIGENCE.**
TURN TO PAGE 43

Yes! That sign warns you of toxic (highly poisonous) substances inside.

REX trundles into the room and sends back an image using its wide-angle camera. Ahead is the Rubik's Cube–shaped shutdown button, but you need to program REX to get there, avoiding any obstacles.

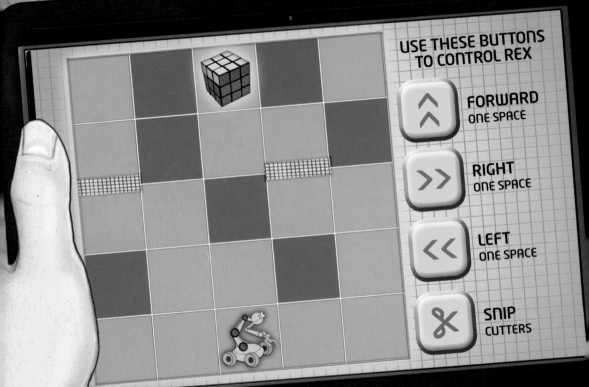

USE THESE BUTTONS TO CONTROL REX

FORWARD ONE SPACE

RIGHT ONE SPACE

LEFT ONE SPACE

SNIP CUTTERS

Which algorithm (set of instructions) do you give to REX?

1

FORWARD, LEFT, FORWARD, LEFT, SNIP, FORWARD, FORWARD.
TRAVEL TO PAGE 36

2

RIGHT, RIGHT, FORWARD, SNIP, LEFT, FORWARD, FORWARD, LEFT, FORWARD.
MOVE TO PAGE 12

3

RIGHT, RIGHT, FORWARD, FORWARD, LEFT, SNIP, FORWARD, LEFT, FORWARD.
GO TO PAGE 38

I have a plan! First, you need to collect REX, my Robotic Extreme eXplorer, from the Deepwater Tank. It can work in dangerous situations.

MARS

Robots like this help us to learn about places that are too dangerous for humans to go—such as into space. Do you know the name of a robot that explores Mars?

CURIOSITY
GO TO PAGE 42

CASSINI-HUYGENS
HEAD OVER TO PAGE 5

VOYAGER 1
TURN TO PAGE 27

Success! The Ocean Navigator dives to a depth of 333 feet (100 meters) unharmed, grabs REX, and surfaces.

You try to turn on the tablet—it's had plenty of time in the light to charge. Engleby appears on the screen.

"Well done! Here's a brain-boggler for you. What's the deepest an underwater robot has ever gone?"

3,300 FEET (1,000 METERS)
GO TO PAGE 37

33,000 FEET (10,000 METERS)
TURN TO PAGE 5

Correct! One invention can often inspire others, and Edison's carbon microphone turned sound into electrical signals. This was useful for lots of inventions, from telephones to radios.

You race into the Inventors' Hall carrying REX under your arm.

You'll love this hall—it's all about inventors! The keys are hidden behind a display of inventions by women.

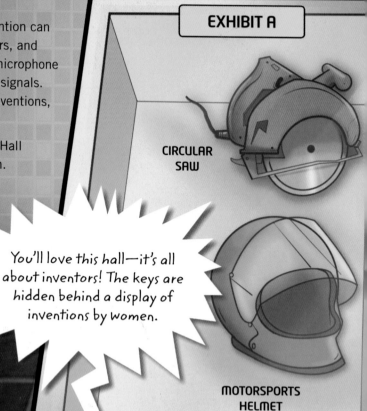

EXHIBIT A

CIRCULAR SAW

MOTORSPORTS HELMET

WINDSHIELD WIPERS

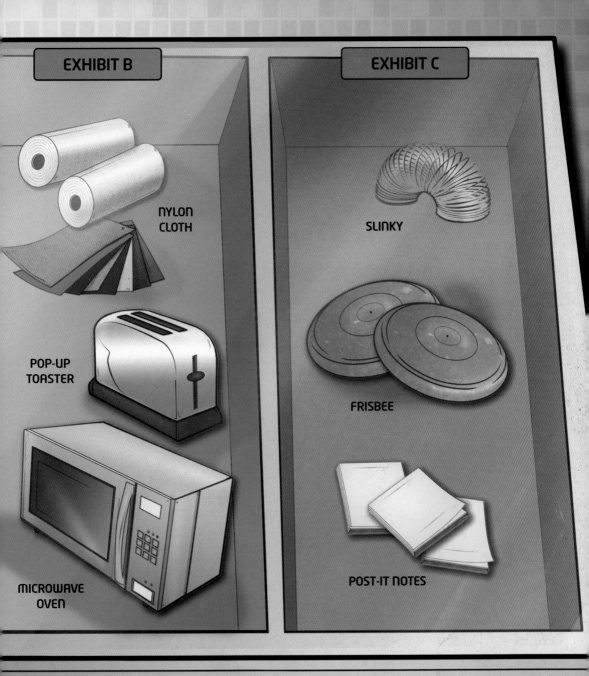

EXHIBIT B

NYLON
CLOTH

POP-UP
TOASTER

MICROWAVE
OVEN

EXHIBIT C

SLINKY

FRISBEE

POST-IT NOTES

Which exhibit are they behind?

A

EXHIBIT A
MOVE TO PAGE 8

B

EXHIBIT B
TRAVEL TO PAGE 39

C

EXHIBIT C
GO TO PAGE 18

Incorrect! Ernő Rubik was born in 1944, so it's a little too soon for his invention!

TRY AGAIN
ON PAGE 8

 Not quite. An AGV is an automated guided vehicle—you were in one earlier! It follows lines or wires on the floor to move around.

GO BACK TO PAGE 16
AND **TRY AGAIN**

 Correct! The number 3 written in binary is **11**.

In the first number **(1)**, the 1 is on the right.

In the second number **(10)**, a 1 can't be added to the right, so the number on the right changes to a 0 and the 1 shifts to the left.

In the third number **(11)**, a 1 can be added to the right because there's a 0 in place.

You follow the route to the **AND/OR/NOT Room**. You press the smart key against the sensor. Three buttons light up with symbols for three types of computer logic gate: **AND, OR,** and **NOT**.

AND/OR/NOT ROOM

 SECURITY CODE

Press symbol for the NOT gate.

Which button do you press?

BUTTON 1
TURN TO PAGE 43

BUTTON 2
FLIP TO PAGE 32

BUTTON 3
GO TO PAGE 12

26

You don't know your space robots, do you? Voyager 1 is a space probe, launched in 1977, to study the outer solar system.

TRY AGAIN
ON PAGE 23

No. The "A" does not stand for amphibious, which means a vehicle that can work on land and in water.

TURN BACK
TO PAGE 43

Correct! End effectors are tools, such as grippers or welding tools, fitted to the end of robot arms.

Ena is so impressed that she asks you to take a new robot for its streamlining test. You rush out and are halfway across the factory floor before you realize that you don't know where to go.

← CAD ROOM

WIND TUNNEL →

You reach some signs.
Which way for a streamlining test?

GO TO THE
CAD ROOM.
JUMP TO PAGE 38

GO TO THE
WIND TUNNEL.
TURN TO PAGE 14

No, pressure sensors would be activated if you touched the robot.

HAVE ANOTHER TRY ON PAGE 30

 If you only activate switch A, the circuit will not be complete.

TRY AGAIN ON PAGE 32

 That's the radioactivity room. It is dangerous, like the poisonous room, but there's no shutdown button in there.

TURN BACK TO PAGE 36

 In front of you is a large robot with two sharp, magnetic metal grippers. On top is a man you've never seen before.

Thought you'd try and stop me, eh? We'll see about that!

How can you protect yourself? There are some steel barrels to your right and some wooden boxes to your left.

Which way do you go?

LEFT GO TO PAGE 38

RIGHT TURN TO PAGE 40

Yes! An **AND** gate will only send a signal if it receives a signal from both of its inputs. This means both switches need to be activated.

The barrier opens and you're inside a corridor with three doors to the Hazmat Cells. Suddenly, the tablet makes a noise and Engleby's face disappears from the screen. Instead, words appear.

ENGLEBY HERE.
ABORT MISSION.
ROBOT EDIE
DISABLED SURGER.
GO TO MAIN DOORS.

It seems odd that Engleby would change his mind so quickly. And who's Edie? Does he mean EDNA? Wait – what if a robot has hacked into the tablet and is trying to trick you!

How do you find out if the message is from Engleby or a robot?

HAVE A **NORMAL** **CONVERSATION.**
GO TO PAGE 36

GO TO THE **MAIN** **DOORS** TO FIND OUT.
HEAD OVER TO PAGE 16

There are more than one million industrial robot arms used for welding, spraying, and many other tasks, but they're not the most common robots.

TRY AGAIN ON PAGE 41

 The claw is good for gripping items that its prongs can dig into, but it cannot hold onto the smooth glass.

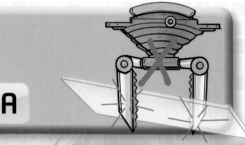

HEAD BACK TO PAGE 8 AND TRY AGAIN A

 Yes, swarm robots are inspired by insects. They can spread out to search an area.

A swarm robot? It must be acting as a spy for our intruders. Work out what kind of sensors it has and find a way to get past it, so it doesn't sound an alarm.

The robot seems to react whenever you make a sound. What kind of sensors does it have?

VISION SENSORS
GO TO PAGE 10

SONIC SENSORS
TURN TO PAGE 18

PRESSURE SENSORS
HEAD OVER TO PAGE 28

Try again! A robot called Dante traveled inside volcanoes in 1993.

RETURN TO PAGE 13 TO GUESS AGAIN

That sign warns of high voltage electricity.

HEAD BACK TO PAGE 36 AND TRY AGAIN

 Pliers could twist the wire onto the panel, but it may fall off.

HAVE ANOTHER TRY ON PAGE 42

No, a robot's sensors aren't part of the drive system. Sensors send information about a robot or its surroundings to the controller. The controller can then command its parts.

GO BACK TO PAGE 21 AND TRY AGAIN

 No, that's a humanoid robot. Most humanoid robots develop from a prototype in their early stages.

GO BACK TO PAGE 39 AND TRY AGAIN

 Try again!

500 gigabytes (GB) is a large amount of computer memory, but it's not the largest here.

GO BACK TO PAGE 12

Yes, that's the **NOT** gate symbol.

The door slides open. Inside the room is a giant electrical circuit with two big switches. Engleby explains what you should do.

BATTERY

LIGHT BULB

DANGER

HAZMAT
CELLS

This is a giant logic gate. If you activate the right switch to complete the circuit, the door to the Hazmat Cells will open. These are small rooms used to test inventions in dangerous situations.

Do you activate switch A, switch B, or both switches?

OFF ON

OFF ON

A
SWITCH A
TURN TO PAGE 28

B
SWITCH B
HEAD OVER TO PAGE 10

AB
BOTH SWITCHES
GO TO PAGE 19

Incorrect! **OR** gates send out a signal if they receive a signal from either of their inputs. A circuit featuring an **OR** gate would have needed only one of the switches to be activated to work.

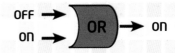

GO BACK TO PAGE 19 AND TRY AGAIN **AB**

Big mistake. Friction is a force generated when two things rub together. The less friction the wheels experience, the faster they can move. The AGV speeds up. Better try something else . . . quickly!

FRICTION

minimum   maximum

GO BACK TO PAGE 14

Just in time! The pneumatic robot uses air through tubes to power its parts. As it loses power, it lurches forward and flings the man through the air—SPLASH—straight into the vat of paint!

You're startled by a hand on your shoulder. It's Engleby and he's delighted.

You've saved the day!

I've alerted the police, so they should be here any minute. But who's behind all of this?

GO TO PAGE 34 TO FIND OUT

The police arrive and pull the man out of the paint tank.
He doesn't seem quite so threatening now!
It's Hugh Reeka—Engleby's former chief designer!

You've ruined me, Engleby! After you fired me, no one wanted me!

You shouldn't have tried to steal my secrets! You should have learned how to invent and solve problems, just like my young apprentice here.
In fact, he deserves a promotion. How would you like to be my personal trainee? I will teach you everything I know.
Yes please!
Great job—you not only met your hero, you also saved his factory and bagged yourself a once-in-a-lifetime job!

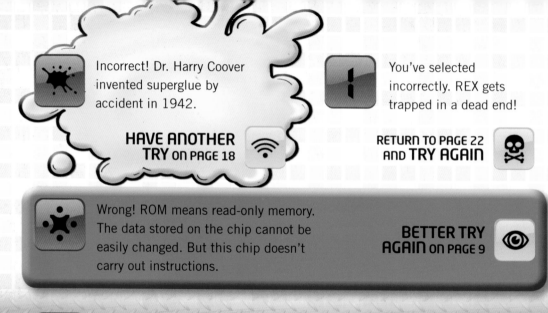

Incorrect! Dr. Harry Coover invented superglue by accident in 1942.

HAVE ANOTHER TRY ON PAGE 18

You've selected incorrectly. REX gets trapped in a dead end!

RETURN TO PAGE 22 AND TRY AGAIN

Wrong! ROM means read-only memory. The data stored on the chip cannot be easily changed. But this chip doesn't carry out instructions.

BETTER TRY AGAIN ON PAGE 9

Yes! You have a text-only conversation and try to work out if you are talking to a human or a robot. You soon realize that you're speaking to a robotic imposter—the bad guys are on to you! You say that you'll come to the main doors straight away. That should buy you some time.

You turn your attention back to the Hazmat Cells. REX needs to enter the room containing poisonous gas to activate the shutdown button. Which room do you choose?

GO TO PAGE 28

HEAD TO PAGE 31

TURN TO PAGE 22

Correct! A terabyte (TB) is equal to 1,000 gigabytes (GB)—more than enough to run the communications program.

The Solar Talking Tablet is finished! With it tucked in your back pocket, you crawl along the ventilation shaft. The shaft splits into three, and each passage is labeled. You contact Engleby for instructions.

> Let's get your gray matter working.
> Follow the passage named after the unit for measuring an electric current.

Which passage do you choose?

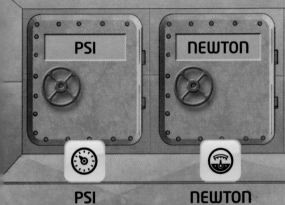

| PSI | NEWTON | AMP |

PSI
TURN TO PAGE 21

NEWTON
JUMP TO PAGE 42

AMP
MOVE ON TO PAGE 10

You're wrong! 3,300 feet (1,000 meters) is easy for a robot designed to withstand the pressure.

RETURN TO PAGE 23 AND PICK AGAIN

No, humanoids are very expensive to produce and the technology is quite new, so there aren't that many around.

HAVE ANOTHER TRY ON PAGE 41

You realize your mistake almost immediately. This robot can dive to great depths, but will take 20 minutes to reach the pod.

PICK A DIFFERENT AUV ON **PAGE 6**

Wrong direction! CAD stands for computer-aided design. Computers are used to help design many inventions, but you need to go elsewhere to see how streamlined an object is.

GO BACK TO PAGE 27 ❈

Poor call. The grippers are powerful and sharp. They slice through the wood.

RETURN TO PAGE 28 👾

Goal! REX reaches its target and grasps part of the Rubik's Cube–shaped button.

Now, you must command REX's gripper to line up the button's front face with all red squares.

Which direction command do you select?

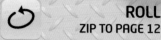

PITCH
GO TO PAGE 43 ↻

YAW
HEAD TO PAGE 20 ↺

ROLL
ZIP TO PAGE 12 ↻

Right decision. Brakes work by generating more friction. More friction slows down the wheels—and just in time. You stop less than a second before crashing!

With all that commotion, you didn't notice that everyone has left. The factory is now eerily quiet, except for two hushed voices nearby.

All staff have fled, Boss. Brilliant idea to make the robots go crazy and scare everyone.

Revenge is sweet! Communications are cut, the Superbots are on patrol, and the Power Surger is charging. In an hour it will fry every electric circuit in the building. It will be the end of Engleby's prototypes and his precious Inventorium!

What's a prototype?

AN EARLY VERSION
OF AN INVENTION,
BUILT FOR TESTING.
TURN TO PAGE 8

★

A FINAL VERSION
OF A ROBOT,
READY FOR WORK.
HEAD OVER TO PAGE 19

🤖

A ROBOT THAT IS
SHAPED AND **WORKS**
LIKE A HUMAN.
GO TO PAGE 31

B No. The microwave oven was invented by Percy Spencer in the 1940s, nylon was discovered by Wallace Carothers in the 1930s, and the pop-up toaster was first devised by Charles Strite in 1919.

HAVE ANOTHER
TRY ON PAGE 24

A glue gun might do the job at first, but it wouldn't hold the wire in place for long.

GO BACK TO
PAGE 42 AND
TRY AGAIN

Good choice! Steel is attracted to magnets and the barrels stick to the blades. It buys you a bit of time, but then the robot shakes off the barrels and comes after you again.

You're trapped down a dead end. There's a giant tank of paint behind you.

You cannot escape the pneumatic power of my mighty machine!

Pneumatic power . . . you need to think of a way to cut the power source.

Which pipe do you pull out of its socket to stop the robot in its tracks?

AIR TANK

FLUID TANK

THE PIPE TO THE
AIR TANK.
GO TO PAGE 33

THE PIPE TO THE
FLUID TANK.
TURN TO PAGE 18

Yes! He made the first prototype out of wood when he was 30 years old.

The door slides open and you find yourself face to face with a robot. Oh no! Is it a Superbot?

INTRUDER ALERT! VERIFY IDENTITY BY ANSWERING QUESTION. WHAT'S THE MOST COMMON TYPE OF ROBOT?

What do you say?

ROBOTIC VACUUM CLEANER
GO TO PAGE 11

INDUSTRIAL ROBOT ARM
FLIP TO PAGE 30

HUMANOID
TURN TO PAGE 37

No, 2 and 5 aren't the numbers used by computers in this way.

TRY AGAIN
ON PAGE 10

 No, James Dyson invented the first bagless vacuum cleaner. He built more than 5,000 prototypes over 15 years before he got it right!

HAVE ANOTHER TRY ON PAGE 5

Yes! The Curiosity rover has been exploring Mars since it landed in 2012. It uses cameras and scientific instruments to record data, which it sends back to Earth.

You need REX because you're going to activate the electricity shutdown button, in a room of poisonous gas. It will cut off the Power Surger and all the electricity in the building before the surger can destroy everything.

You'll have to go alone because I can't fit in the ventilation shaft—the only way out of here! But, in a way, I'll be with you—with my prototype Solar Talking Tablet. It's almost finished. I just need to join the power wire to the solar panel. Could you pass me the correct tool please?

Which tool do you pass?

SOLDERING IRON
TURN TO PAGE 12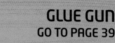

GLUE GUN
GO TO PAGE 39

PLIERS
FLIP TO PAGE 31

 Wrong! Force, not electric current, is measured in newtons.

 Wrong. 3 is the right answer in the decimal number system you normally use—but not in the binary system, which only uses the numbers 1 and 0.

TURN BACK
TO PAGE 37

HEAD BACK TO PAGE 17
AND **TRY AGAIN**

No, pitch is the wrong direction.

ROTATE PITCH

TRY AGAIN ON PAGE 38

TRY AGAIN ON PAGE 38

 Wrong! A robot's intelligence to make decisions comes from its controller, which runs computer programs created by people.

HAVE ANOTHER TRY ON PAGE 21

HAVE ANOTHER TRY ON PAGE 21

 No, that's the symbol for an **AND** gate. A **NOT** gate has just one signal coming in and one signal leaving it.

GO BACK TO PAGE 26

GO BACK TO PAGE 26

Correct! Velcro is now used as a fastener for clothes, shoes, and many other products.

The tablet begins a message but then goes into sleep mode. The solar panels must have lost too much power in the dark ventilation shaft. You'll have to figure this one out for yourself while it recharges. You managed to hear:

SLEEP MODE

TO RETRIEVE REX, USE AN AUV...

What does AUV stand for?

IT'S AN **AUTONOMOUS UNDERWATER VEHICLE.** GO TO PAGE 13

IT'S AN **AUTONOMOUS UNDERWATER VEHICLE.** GO TO PAGE 13

IT'S AN **AMPHIBIOUS UNDERWATER VEHICLE.** TURN TO PAGE 27

IT'S AN **AMPHIBIOUS UNDERWATER VEHICLE.** TURN TO PAGE 27

GLOSSARY

AGV (automated guided vehicle)
A machine that travels by itself along a path in a factory or other building.

Alloy
A material that is a mixture of different metals or a metal containing other substances.

Amp
The unit used to measure the strength of an electric current.

AUV (autonomous underwater vehicle)
An underwater robot that can work by itself and find its own way through water.

Bar (depth)
A unit of measurement used when calculating air or water pressure. Also measured in pounds per square inch (PSI).

Byte
A unit used to measure computer information. It is equal to eight bits, which is the smallest unit used to store information on a computer.

CAD (computer-aided design)
The use of powerful computers to help design all the parts of a product, such as a car or DVD player.

Controller
The part of a robot that makes decisions and tells the other parts of the robot what to do. It is usually a computer.

CPU (central processing unit)
One or more silicon chips that act as the "brains" of a computer and help it to perform its basic tasks.

A CPU (left) can be as small as a fingernail!

Degrees of freedom

The different directions in which a robot can move, for example up and down, left and right, and forward and backward.

Drive system

A collection of parts in a robot that together allow the robot to move.

Electric current

The measure of how much electric charge flows through an electrical circuit. The more electric charge that flows, the bigger the current.

End effector

A device or tool, such as a gripping hand, connected to the end of a robot arm.

Friction

A force that prevents one surface from sliding easily over another surface.

Hazmat

Short for hazardous materials, substances that are poisonous or harmful to living things.

Humanoid

A robot that looks like or acts in similar ways to a human being.

This robot arm has six degrees of freedom: up/down, forward/backward, left/right, pitch, yaw, and roll.

Industrial

Relating to industry—where raw materials (such as crude oil or coal) are processed and made into finished goods or parts, often in factories.

Inventor

A person who creates a new item, such as a new type of machine, or develops new ways of doing things.

Logic gate

Microscopic switches or circuits in electronics that help computers and other devices make decisions.

MAV (micro air vehicle)

A small flying robot.

Pneumatic

A drive system in a robot (or other machine) that uses air or another gas under pressure in tubes to move parts.

Prototype

The first experimental form of a new machine's design, used to test the design before it is produced. A number of prototypes are usually made before the final product can be produced.

PSI (pounds per square inch)

A unit of measurement used when calculating air or water pressure. Also measured in Bar.

Radioactivity

Radioactive substances give out radiation particles. At high levels, these can damage living tissue and cause health problems.

RAM (random-access memory)

The memory used by a computer when it is working on tasks or making calculations.

Robot

A machine that can work from the information it collects, or can be programmed to carry out complicated work and tasks.

This is a prototype of a 3D printer (a machine that makes prototypes!).

A very hot tool called a soldering iron is used to melt solder for joining metals together.

ROM (read-only memory)

A type of computer memory that acts as a permanent store. Once information is placed and stored in ROM, it cannot be erased.

Sensor

A device that collects information about a robot or its surroundings. Sensors can, for example, detect movement, sound, and heat.

Silicon chip

A collection of tiny electronic circuits etched onto a small wafer of silicon material. It is used to store and process information in computers.

Solar panels

Panels containing special cells that convert sunlight into electricity.

Solder

A mixture of metals, such as tin and lead, which are melted and used to join metal parts together.

Spacecraft

A vehicle that is sent into space to explore or to carry supplies.

Streamlining

To design and shape an object or machine so that air or water flows as smoothly around it as possible.

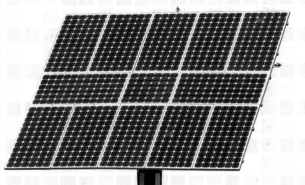

Solar panels are angled toward the sun to collect as much sunlight as possible.

Taking it further

The Rubik's Quest series is designed to motivate children to develop their Science, Technology, Engineering, and Mathematics (STEM) skills. They will learn how to apply their know-how to the world through engaging adventure stories involving the Rubik's Cube, a mind-bending puzzle used throughout the world by people of all ages. For each book, readers must solve a series of problems to make progress toward the exciting conclusion.

The books do not follow a conventional pattern. The reader is directed to jump forward and backward through the book according to the answers they give to the problems. If their answers are correct, the reader progresses to the next part of the story; if they are incorrect the reason is explained, before the reader is directed back to try the problem again. Additional support may be found in the glossary at the back of the book.

To support your child's development you can:

- Read the book with your child.

- Solve the initial problems and discover how the book works.

- Continue reading with your child until he or she is using the book confidently, following the **"GO TO"** instructions to find the next puzzle or explanation.

- Encourage your child to read on alone. Ask "What's happening now?" Prompt your child to tell you how the story develops and what problems they have solved.

- Look up an interesting invention with your child. Learn about the inventor and the challenges he or she had to overcome to succeed.

- Create a simple "match the inventor to the inventions" challenge using a library book or the Internet.

- Become inventors by drawing your own designs for new vehicles or household appliances.

- Go online to investigate robots such as AUVs or flying robots.

- Make a humanoid robot costume together. Play at programming this robot and discuss what voice commands the robot would need to pick up an apple and pass it to you.

- Have fun thinking about what future robots might look like and what they might do.

- Most of all, make learning fun!